THE
BRYNGWYN

It was to have been the main line, part of the grand scheme of 1872 to construct a network of eight narrow gauge lines to link most of the major places in North Wales. It ended up as a rather esoteric branch of the only one of the eight lines to have been constructed.

This then is the story of the main line that never was. Its problems, its characters, its workings and its final incarnation as a delightful footpath along which one may wander today imagining the bustle and clank of slate wagons, the whistle of the locomotive and the characteristic beat of a narrow gauge engine as it tackled the 1 in 40 grade.

By

John Keylock & Dave Southern

This book is dedicated to the memory of John Keylock who was the inspiration behind the restoration of Tryfan Junction station which was to lead to the conversion of the trackbed of the Bryngwyn Branch to a permissive public footpath.

Others can now enjoy the delights of the former branch by walking in the footsteps of those early narrow gauge railway pioneers.

Contents

1) Author's Preface

T HE IDEA OF a book on the Bryngwyn Branch was conceived when working on the restoration of the station building at Tryfan Junction during April 2011. One of the jobs that day was the installation of two wooden posts to accept an information panel about Tryfan Junction and the Bryngwyn branch which had been reincarnated as a 'Slate Trail/permissive footpath'.

Today's Welsh Highland Railway is more than a seasonal tourist attraction providing a car-free means of appreciating Snowdonia. The railway is a public transport system which can take the walker to a variety of destinations particularly for the ascent of Snowdon, a facility first provided by the North Wales Narrow Gauge Railway in 1881.

Therefore this is rather more than a branch line treatise, as it gives a description of the walker's route to the top of the Bryngwyn Incline from where the quarry remains on Moel Tryfan can be viewed but be warned not to stray beyond the fence as the quarries are dangerous and private property.   There is the opportunity to continue into the Nantlle Valley or drop back down to the Gwyrfai

The notice board at Tryfan Junction that inspired this book. This photograph was taken on the 21st May 2011, the day that the slate trail was officially opened from Tryfan Junction to Rhostryfan.

David Allan

valley further south; at Waenfawr, Salem or Plas-y-Nant where trains stop, or do so, on request.

The majority of historical photographs have come from the extensive Welsh Highland Railway Heritage Group collection which has been accumulated over the last 40 years. Thanks are due to those who have provided additional photographs and proof read this publication as it has evolved but nevertheless any errors that have slipped through the net are the sole responsibility of the writers.

During the operational life of the branch, photography was not today's popular activity and the branch was very much "off the beaten track". Consequently, photographs are rare so we make no apology for reproducing some of indifferent quality.

Photographers, where known, are credited. This book has been funded by the Welsh Highland Railway Heritage Group with the profits from its sale going towards the on-going restoration of the Tryfan Junction station building, the whole station site and its subsequent maintenance.

This photograph of the newly re-constructed Tryfan Junction station undertaken by the Welsh Highland Railway Heritage Group shows progress on a wet day in November 2012
David Allan

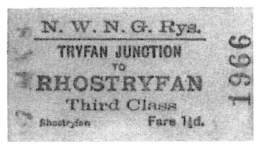

2) Historical Background

B Y 1870, ALL the major slate producing areas in North West Wales had rail access with the exception of the Moel Tryfan quarries. However, a network of two foot gauge railways was proposed that would remedy this situation.

The promoters were quarry and land owners who had both influence and standing in the area. So, rather late in the day the grandiose North Wales Narrow Gauge Railways (NWNGR) scheme was born.

In 1872 the North Wales Narrow Gauge Railways Bill was presented to Parliament and at one of several parliamentary committees Sir Llewelyn Turner, Chairman of the promotional Board of Directors, gave evidence in favour of the scheme. He said, "It would open up the district between Corwen and Caernarfon, Portmadoc and Betws-y-Coed by railway communication. If the railways are made an extensive trade will be created in the Caernarfon District in iron ore; additional slate quarries will be worked and a considerable trade in flags will come into existence currently prevented by the want of means of transit". Sir Llewelyn also pointed out that part of the planned railways would be of importance in helping the population of the Snowdon District with the means of getting to Caernarfon market. Tourist traffic was also anticipated. In August 1872 the NWNGR Bill received the Royal Assent.

Charles Easton Spooner (left) & Sir Lewlleyn Turner (right)

FR Archives

Thus came into being the General, Portmadoc to Betws-y-Coed and Moel Tryfan Undertakings of the NWNGR with separate share capitals. The Moel Tryfan Undertaking's share issue prospectus offered 6,600 shares at £10 each for a line commencing at a junction with the Caernarvonshire Railway at what became Dinas Junction, to Bryngwyn and Rhyd Ddu. An agreement was already in place to lease the line to Hugh Beaver Roberts, - owner of Braich Quarry on Moel Tryfan - for 21 years. However, this agreement was soon to be revoked.

The share prospectus emphasised the success of the Festiniog Railway and suggested that a similar success in operating the undertaking would enable a 10% dividend to be paid to shareholders. Consulting engineer to the scheme was Charles Easton Spooner, the son of James Spooner, who engineered the Festiniog Railway (FR).

At the first half yearly meeting of the company in March 1873, it was reported that the majority of shares had been spoken for and that a contract to construct the Moel Tryfan Undertaking had been awarded to Hugh Unsworth McKie who anticipated completion in 12 months. Two years on and the lines remained incomplete due mainly to the time spent in arbitration between McKie and Spooner.

McKie was retained, took on more men and was instructed to direct his efforts to the completion of the railway line to Bryngwyn. However, the contract with McKie, which had cost the company dear in both time and money, was terminated in February 1876 and G. M. Boys was appointed in his stead.

James Cholomedy Russell - Receiver and General Manager of the line until 1912. **(Nick Booker collection)**

The line opened for goods traffic from Dinas to Tryfan Junction and Bryngwyn on the 21st May 1877, for passengers on the 15th August 1877, and settled down to its main business of slate conveyance. The branch was designated as the main line with its mile posts being measured from Dinas to Bryngwyn whilst the measurements to Rhyd Ddu began at Tryfan Junction confirming the branch's initial 'main line' status. Unfortunately, trade did not reach expectations and in 1878 the railway went into receivership with James Cholmeley Russell appointed as Receiver - a situation that would endure for the whole of the line's existence.

When the small but potentially profitable Bryngwyn branch opened it was, like the rest of the railway, well endowed with staff;

Bryngwyn, Rhostryfan and Tryfan Junction all boasted their own stationmaster! This situation was inevitably short lived with the railway in receivership and the demand for slate in free fall.

Two locomotives, 'Moel Tryfan' and 'Snowdon Ranger' were delivered in 1876, while 'Beddgelert', (with its inclined boiler) was specifically designed to work the steeply graded and tightly curved Bryngwyn Branch, was delivered in 1878.

Three 4-wheeled and two bogie brake composite carriages were delivered for the railway's initial opening; with three 6-wheeled vehicles arriving in 1878. These latter vehicles were of Cleminson's flexible wheelbase design and they would have been ideal for working the Bryngwyn section but alas there is no photographic record of such usage.

Other potential schemes under NWNGR auspices included extending the line to Caernarfon, thus avoiding slate trans-shipment at Dinas, and replacing the Bryngwyn incline with an adhesion-worked spiral - neither materialised. Likewise, it was only with the advent of the Welsh Highland Railway (W.H.R) in 1922 that any part of the General Undertaking became a reality.

During the 1880's business was also good for the inward carriage of coal, lime, and other quarry goods as well as the community requirements for Rhostryfan, Bryngwyn, Rhosgadfan, Carmel and Fron. However, the line remained essentially dependant on the slate trade

One of the NWNGR's 'Gloucester' Cleminson coaches built in 1878 and photographed in use as a store at Dinas in 1934.
This coach would have been ideal for use on the branch, but alas there is no record of such service.
Roger Kidner

and when there was a downturn in the slate industry the finances of the line suffered.

With the coming of the First World War passenger numbers declined and quarries closed. Coaches were left in sidings and deteriorated. Slate wagons filled the yards as there was no work and no men to repair the damaged ones. One engine in steam was introduced and the signalling system was no longer needed. Track maintenance became minimal and sleepers rotted. In 1916 men employed in quarrying no longer enjoyed protected status and therefore became liable for war service.

Passenger traffic ceased on the 31st December 1913 - never to be reinstated. Slate traffic, along with coal and groceries, continued until the whole undertaking was absorbed into the WHR in 1921. Freight traffic continued with the last slate consignment coming down the incline from Moel Tryfan Quarry in February 1935.

Top

The right hand train shows "Beddgelert" with her carriages awaiting departure from Dinas Junction in 1894. The carriage immediately behind the locomotive is a Cleminson 6-wheeler of 1878 vintage.
The standard gauge track (left in picture) is still a single line and provided a cross platform interchange for LNWR services between Caernarfon and Afon Wen.

Left
Dinas to Rhostryfan 'Parliamentary' ticket

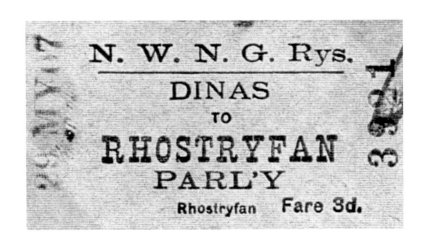

3) Route Described - Infrastructure & Signalling

Tryfan Junction

IN THE ORIGINAL 'grand design' the junction made the bold and optimistic statement that the area's future lay in slate. The location has always been remote, serving two near-by farms – one of which, Tyddyn Gwydd – provided the colloquial name for the junction.

Built by the mid-1870s, in typical vernacular style, the dressed stone exterior conceals a basic rubble stone construction, plastered inside. With its hipped roof the building is 30 ft long, 18 ft 6 ins wide, and 9 ft 6 ins to the eaves. Today's reconstruction is faithful to its 'as built' external appearance. The layout of the junction is best illustrated by the accompanying plans.

'Palmerston' with FR stock photographed at Tryfan Junction in 1923 on the re-opening day.

The roof of the signal box is just visible; the railwayman on the opposite platform is seen holding the staff.

TRYFAN JUNCTION c 1889

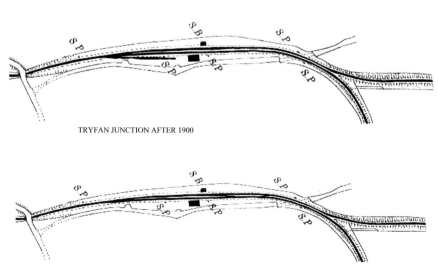

TRYFAN JUNCTION AFTER 1900

Track diagrams
Upper shows the junction in 1889 - note the siding to the left.

Lower is the diagram after 1900 - the siding has been removed and a crossover is now in place.

Top - Tryfan Junction in 1942 with the demolition train appearing to have come off the branch. The rotten sleepers are loaded onto a coach chassis. The station sign and the characteristic telegraph pole which had stood in front of the building have disappeared.
A.E. Rimmer

Middle - Tryfan Junction in 1947 after the track had been lifted and nature takes over with the building falling into disrepair
Bill Rear

Lower - Tryfan Junction, its reconstruction nearing completion by the Welsh Highland Heritage Group in 2013. The platform is being extended in front of the building; the plank across the centre is to gain the correct level.
Dave Southern

Leaving Tryfan Junction the branch immediately starts curving to the right, through 180° at 3¾ chains radius and on a long 1 in 39 gradient, through a cutting and into a straight with the track now going in the opposite direction to the main line. The line then dives under a road bridge and over the Afon Rhyd. Both bridges are characteristically N.W.N.G.R with yellow brick arches. It crosses two further streams then climbs through open fields at 1 in 48 until Rhostryfan is reached.

Top
First bridge on the branch out of Tryfan Junction with the lane to Rhostryfan being carried over the line by a typical NWNGR structure with a yellow brick arch.
David Allan

Left
The lane (left in the photo) to Tyddyn Gwydd, the farm from which the local name for the station is derived, is the original trackbed while a new footpath (right in the photo) has been created alongside to a point approximately 200 yards distant where it joins the original trackbed
Dave Southern

Top - Rhostryfan station derelict in 1947 showing its proximity to the village. The door gave access to the gent's urinal; the window in the rear elevation was divided internally to provide light for both ladies and gents lavatories.
W.A. Camwell

Left -A distant view of Rhostryfan station in the open landscape surrounding the village.
Michael Whitehouse

Bottom - Front elevation of Rhostryfan station with the nameboard still clinging to the wall

Rhostryfan

Rhostryfan was the only intermediate station on the Branch, 70 chains distant from Tryfan Junction and 482 feet above sea level, it boasted a standard NWNGR design station building and was located very close to the centre of the community which it served with a weigh house at the station entrance. There was a single siding for coal traffic with a goods warehouse that was later replaced by a loading platform. Access to the siding was controlled from a lever frame on a stone base.

On leaving the station, the line passed over an access lane followed by a bridge over the Afon Dwyld before entering a

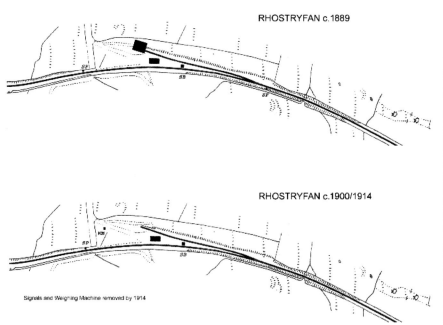

RHOSTRYFAN c.1889

RHOSTRYFAN c.1900/1914

Signals and Weighing Machine removed by 1914

Top - Rhostryfan station in 1941, the year before the track was lifted. The ladies - Mrs Bolton (left and Mrs Boyd-Carpenter (right) are sitting on the remains of a ganger's trolley.
J.F. Bolton

Middle - layout at Rhostryfan in 1889

Lower - layout at Rhostryfan in 1900- 1914. Signals and weighing machine had been removed by 1914.

cutting and passing under a unique accommodation footbridge. Then followed a jack-arch bridge with a rectangular opening carrying Rhostryfan High Street over the railway. From here the line meanders between houses and fields before crossing a minor road and into an area of open moorland, following the contours of the hillside with gentle curves. A 90º curve brought the line to the Bryngwyn road crossing followed by an embankment on a 180º curve with a 2 ¾ chain radius around Bryngwyn Farm. Bryngwyn station was reached after crossing the Rhosgadfan to Carmel road on the skew.

Top - Trackbed passes under Rhostryfan High Street by means of a rectangular jack-arch bridge. **(Bill Rear 1948).**

Middle - Looking down Rhostryfan High Street from the bridge that carried the road over the railway. **(Commercial post card - collection Peter Johnson).**

Lower - Site of Rhostryfan station in 2013 marked by a replica station sign and platform. Picnic tables have been provided for walkers from which good views may be obtained of Ynys Mon (Anglesey). **Stuart McNair**

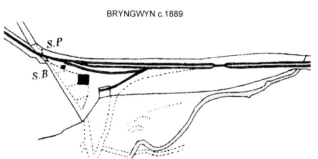

BRYNGWYN c.1889

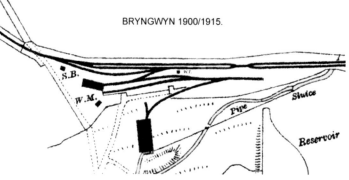

BRYNGWYN 1900/1915.

Bryngwyn

At 650 feet above sea level Bryngwyn station was 2 miles 35 chains from Tryfan Junction and located at the bottom of the Bryngwyn incline. By 1900 the buildings comprised a standard NWNGR station building, goods shed, and signal box located just beyond the road crossing. The site also boasted one of the few locomotive water towers on the system - located between the goods loop and the head shunt.

There was no actual village at Bryngwyn but it was within walking distance from the villages of Rhosgadfan, Y Fron and Carmel.

The site contained a goods loop at the bottom of the incline for slate traffic together with a separate passenger loop off which led to a siding to the goods shed. The coal siding in later years was extended

Top - The rails approach Bryngwyn station from the direction of Rhostryfan. The base of the signal cabin can still be seen in the foreground whilst the station building seems reasonably complete.
Roger Kidner

Lower (left) - the Bryngwyn layout in 1889 and (right) the more sophisticated layout after 1900.

to accommodate a goods loading platform, This in turn led to the head shunt which terminated near the bottom of the incline.

From the head shunt, a further siding led to Bryngwyn Mill powered by a water wheel fed by a pipe from a sluice in the adjacent reservoir. J I C Boyd refers to it as a gunpowder store but its closeness to the station throws doubt on this. By 1893 the mill was being leased by William and John Morris Jones and Inigo Jones. The latter business is still operational beside the Penygroes bypass. It is known that the mill produced writing slates but slate for these did not come from Moel Tryfan quarries but from further afield and delivered by train. (See invoice on page 23).

In 1930 there were three coal merchants operating from the coal-yard at Bryngwyn. Two went by the name of Jones and another was named Griffiths. At the time it cost £1-6-0 to have 6 tons of coal delivered from Dinas and trade must have been good as every home would have had a coal fire!

The bent and twisted rails at the bottom of the Bryngwyn incline stand in mute testimony to the battering they had received during their working life. In the background stands the remains of Bryngwyn station building with abandoned wheels and wagons littering the site.
J.F. Bolton

Bryngwyn station sign - now resides in the Narrow Gauge Railway Museum at Tywyn.

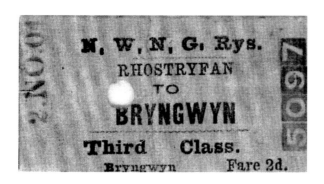

Top
Bryngwyn station is slowly being 'reclaimed', the original building stones no doubt being recycled for more immediate purposes.
Michael Whitehouse

Middle
Long time resident of Rhostryfan, Nesta Williams and her dog Foxy, pose by the level crossing gate that protected the railway from the road at the the throat of Bryngwyn station. Behind the gate the trackbed disappears in the direction of Rhostryfan.
David Allan

Left
Rhostryfan to Bryngwyn Ticket

Left
The double-tracked Bryngwyn incline heads up the hill beyond the water tower. A rake of slate wagons, some empty whilst others appear to be loaded with slate waste, stand forlornly in the left hand siding.
Roger Kidner

Bottom - The Rhosgadfan road crosses the incline on a new bridge, an older bridge can just be seen through the arch
Bill Rear

Drumhead

The double track incline rose at 1 in 10 to 895 feet above sea level and was half a mile long. It was intersected by a minor public road and the Afon Llifon before passing under the Rhosgadfan to Fron road bridge built of slate slab with old rail used for the parapets.

Still climbing the incline traversed a cutting, then an embankment before passing over a small bridge to reach the drum-house. This housed the winding gear for the incline. At just 5 miles and 9 chains from Dinas junction the Drumhead represented the limit of NWGNR jurisdiction. Beyond lay a network of four (later five) feeder lines which served the various quarries in the area. Within a small yard each line had its own loop that provided a run round for the wagons of slate ready for dispatch.

Permanent Way

Initially the 1 ft 11½ ins running line was laid in 35lbs/yard flat-bottomed iron rail in 24ft lengths spiked to the sleepers laid at approximately 2' 6" centres or closer at rail joints. The sleepers were half round section in larch and measured approximately 4 ft 6 ins x 9 ins x 4 ½ ins. This 'way' did not prove to be very permanent and by the mid-1880s a programme of track replacement using 41¼ lb rail in 30' lengths had been initiated. Furthermore, to prevent the track gauge spreading, particularly on curves, 'anti-spread' bars were fixed between sleepers. These had been designed by Robert Livesey – the railway's first 'General Manager' – who also introduced a better method of spiking the flat-bottomed rail to the replacement sleepers.

Signalling

For the opening of the branch signalling contractors, McKenzie and Holland of Worcester provided what turned out to be over elaborate arrangements. Tryfan Junction boasted a modified example of their 'Type 3' design. It was the largest such structure on the whole NWNGR system measuring 15ft x 10ft 6ins and 13ft to the roof ridge. The frame had twenty levers – with one spare – to control seven signals and five points. This number of levers would have provided for point and signal inter locking. The 'country stone' base of the box survives opposite the station building and in the future may well have a replica box built on it.

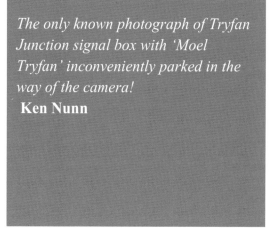

The only known photograph of Tryfan Junction signal box with 'Moel Tryfan' inconveniently parked in the way of the camera!
Ken Nunn

With only one point, and at the most three signals to operate, Rhostryfan would only have required a ground frame albeit probably enclosed. Bryngwyn had an eight lever frame based in a box at the station throat. (See photograph on page 17 that shows the remains of the box)

Signals were of the single spectacle type showing a white light for clear with a blue spectacle back light.

Despite the aforegoing, the Branch was always operated on the principle of 'one engine in steam' so the signalling had fallen into disuse by WWI - the posts being eventually removed when the WHR came on the scene in 1922/23. These posts were of pitch pine with a braced cross on the base necessitating a substantial hole for their initial installation.

Subsequently, at Tryfan Junction, weighted points were set for the main line and locked with a key attached to the train staff. The branch approach to the junction was controlled by a stop board, where trains stopped dead. With a clear path to Dinas confirmed by telephone; staffs were exchanged and the train entered the loop, the points being reset for the main line before proceeding.

4) Passenger Services

IT IS INTERESTING to reflect that a passenger service survived on the branch from 1877 to 1913 whereas on the subsequent WHR it was only from 1922 to 1936. This was chiefly due to the rising popularity of the motor bus which offered a better service in terms of speed and regularity. However until WWI the branch service provided a means for those living in the widely scattered communities to get to Dinas and thus Caernarfon. Timetables and tickets used during the period provide a background to the service offered as there is but one photograph of a train on the branch (page 23). Its two carriages suggest that these were adequate to cater for available traffic – even on Caernarfon market days!

Down	Parly		SO	SX		SO
Dinas	7:20 am	9.58 am	12.30 pm	3.03 pm	5.03 pm	7.43 pm
Tryfan Jct	7:30 am	10.08 am	12.40 pm	3.13 pm	5.13 pm	7.53 pm
Rhostryfan	7:40 am	10.13 am	12.45 pm	3.18 pm	5.18 pm	7.58 pm
Bryngwyn	7.55 am	10.22 am	12.55 pm	3.27 pm	5.27 pm	8.05 pm

Up	Parly		SO	SX	Parly	SO
Bryngwyn	8:30 am	11.50 am	1.40 pm	4.30 pm	6.25 pm	8.30 pm
Rhostryfan	8:40 am	12.00 am	1.50 pm	4.40 pm	6.35 pm	8.40 pm
Tryfan Jct	8:50 am	12:10 pm	2.00 pm	4.50 pm	6.45 pm	8.50 pm
Dinas	8.58 am	12.18 pm	2.08 pm	5.00 pm	6.55 pm	9.00 pm

SO = Saturday only;   SX = Saturday excepted;   Parly = Parliamentary

From at least 1881, by which time the whole railway was open for business, a register of tickets sold at Tryfan Junction was maintained by the station master there.   From said register it is known that a third class single to Rhostryfan cost ½d or 1½d to Bryngwyn.   At the same period a first class return to Rhostryfan cost 4d.   By the first decade of the twentieth century the singles mentioned had increased to 1½d and 3d respectively and a Caernarfon market return – from the junction – was 8d.   All trains offered both 1st and 3rd class accommodation, and Parliamentary fares were available on the first train in each direction essentially for the benefit of workman.

The above timetable is dated February 1878

It will be noted that 'up' and 'down' trains are the reverse of what they became in WHR days.

*Left
Rhostryfan to Dinas 'Parliamentary' ticket*

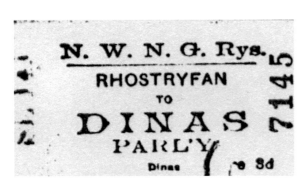

N. W. N. G. Rys.
RHOSTRYFAN
TO
DINAS
PARL'Y
Dinas   8d
7145

Down		SO		SO	SO
Dinas	9.55 am	12.48 pm	3.10 pm	5.25 pm	7.00 pm
Tryfan Jct	10.03 am	12.56 pm	3.18 pm	5.34 pm	7.09 pm
Tryfan Jct	10.08 am	12.58 pm	3.20 pm	5.36 pm	7.10 pm
Rhostryfan	10.15 am	1.04 pm	3.25 pm	5.42 pm	7.15 pm
Bryngwyn	10.25 am	1.14 pm	3.35 pm	5.52 pm	7.25 pm

Up		SO	SO	SX	SO	SO
Bryngwyn	11.30 am	2.00 pm	4.28 pm	5.34 pm	6.00 pm	7.27 pm
Rhostryfan	11.40 am	2.10 pm	4.38 pm	5.44 pm	6.10 pm	7.35 pm
Tryfan Jct	11.45 am	2.15 pm	4.44 pm	5.49 pm	6.15 pm	7.40 pm
Tryfan Jct	11.48 am	2.16 pm	4.45 pm	5.50 pm	6.16 pm	7.40 pm
Dinas	11.58 am	2.25 pm	4.54 pm	6.00 pm	6.26 pm	7.50 pm

SO = Saturdays only; SX = Saturdays excepted

Top - Two-coach passenger train at Bryngwyn circa 1912. The nearer coach is the 'Workmans' whilst the farther vehicle is one of two Pickering Brake Composites supplied to the railway in 1908

Below - the June 1909 passenger timetable

In 1923/24 there was a proposal to restore the branch passenger service using a Simplex tractor and single brake/composite carriage. In view of the gradients involved the Ministry of Transport insisted on continuous brakes but as it was not possible to fit the tractor with an exhauster the proposal came to nought.

By June 1909 the Monday to Friday service was reduced to two trains each way per day with the first departure from Dinas at 9.55am, splitting at Tryfan Junction with the branch service proceeding to Bryngwyn and the main line service to Snowdon (Rhyd Ddu). On the return the trains joined together at Tryfan Junction with the exception of the 5.34 service from Bryngwyn which ran straight through to Dinas.

On a Saturday there were five services each way with passengers changing trains at Dinas for Caernarfon.

S.E. Tyrwhitt's letter of instruction to D.O. Jones, station master at Dinas, re the reduced winter service on the branch.

Septr 20th   23

Mr D.O.Jones,

    Dinas.

Dear Sir,

                    Winter Train Service
                    ─────────────────

        I herewith enclose a printers copy of the proposed timetable for your information. Please consider the Guards workings so far as you are concerned from Octr 1st.

        We find that during Octrober it will be necessary to work the Bryngwyn Branch with the train engine that arrived there at 1/55pm and we propose toshew it on the working timetable to leave Dinas at 2/15pm Bryngwyn arr 3/0pm, leave at 4/15pm Dinas arr 4/55pm. The

        From Novr 1st an engine will be available to go at 11AM and be back at the usual time.

                            Yours faithfully.
                            for S.E.Tyrwhitt

5) An Exchange of Letters

TESTS OF PETROL TRACTOR ON WELSH HIGHLAND RAILWAY.

connection with the article published in the *Railway Gazette* d October 26, 1923, a photograph is reproduced showing a .p. "Simplex" tractor, as used on the light railways of France ng the war period, hauling a test train on the Festiniog Railway ortmadoc, on its way to the Welsh Highland Railway, where it recently subjected to exhaustive trials. It is not anticipated that tractor can be used to replace the ordinary trains, but it may be al for miscellaneous duties or special trips, or for light goods fic. The route over which it was tested involves severe gradients, including an almost unbroken stretch of four miles at 1 in 40 combination with numerous curves of considerable severity.

On the occasion of the trials in question (which we were enal to attend), except for an interval when the tractor required attent mainly due to the fact that the driver had not obtained the c petence which will result from experience, the tractor acquit itself well, making the return journey from Dinas Junction Portmadoc, including a trip on the Bryngwyn branch (which has gradients of 1 in 40), with only one or two service stops.

FOLLOWING THE RE-OPENING of the railway in 1923 it rapidly became clear that substantial savings would have to made if the railway was to become viable. One of the areas exercising the management's attention was the cost of running the Bryngwyn Branch.

One of the options that the ever resourceful Col Stephens considered was using a reconditioned WWI petrol 'Tractor' to operate the trains. He had purchased one of these for shunting duties on the Festiniog Railway and its performance obviously impressed both him and Jack - who was was still General Manager of the Welsh Highland.

Fortunately the exchange of letters that passed between him and the Ministry of Transport have survived. These remarkable letters show Stephens trying to persuade the Ministry that it be of little or no consequence if the then braking regulations were bent a little combined with a scarcely veiled threat that if he didn't get his way then passenger services would be withdrawn. The Ministry however were having none of it and eventually the Colonel gave up his attempt, but not without having one last little nibble at the subject in early March 1924.

The letters show the railway management's thoughts, their concerns and their decision making process at the time.

The above cutting from the Railway Gazette of 1923 reports on the trials of the WWI petrol tractor that. as the following correspondence shows, the management wished to introduce on the branch in order to reduce running costs.

M/963/ED   4th January,   24

The Assistant Secretary,
    Secretarial Department,
        Ministry of Transport,
            6, Whitehall Gardens,
                LONDON, S.W.1.

Sir,

        The passenger traffic on the Welsh Highland Section
of the Railway is very small during the Winter months, and
the few trains that we do run are run at a serious loss.

        It would save the Company a considerable amount
if the passenger trains could be worked by a Simplex Tractor
instead of by a Steam Locomotive.

        We have a Simplex Tractor, 40 H.P., which we
use for shunting purposes at Portmadoc. I have experimented
with this tractor with two ordinary Bogie Coaches (empty),
weighing about 4 tons each, between Portmadoc and Beddgelert (8
and with one coach Beddgelert + Dinas (13 mile)
miles), and found that it could work easily at 15 miles
per hour, which is the maximum speed allowed.

        I am anxious to keep the few passenger trains
running on this section of the railway during the Winter,
but having to work the trains by steam locos., I am afraid
I shall have to discontinue doing so owing to the loss, and
if I do discontinue the service, some inconvenience will
be caused to the public.
        I have been away since 1916 until last April

This series of letters from Welsh Highland Heritage Group archives sheds some fascinating light on the ambitions of the line's superintendent, Capt.John May, to run the branch with a 'tractor' shortly after the WHR re-opened.

-2-

WELSH HIGHLAND RAILWAY (Light Railway) COMPANY.   Sheet No.2.

Assistant Secretary,   4. 1. 1924.
    Ministry of Transport.
    ----

in the Army.   I was very well used to the petrol tractors

during the War, but I am not very conversant with the recent

Ministry of Transport Regulations dealing with the working

of Light Railways.

          I shall be much obliged if you will kindly inform

me if it would be permissable to use a Simple Tractor to work

a passenger train similar to the following:-

                    "The train will not, at any time, consist
                    "of more than one vehicle attached to the Tractor.
                    "It would be a combined Bogie vehicle weighing
                    "about 4 tons, properly fitted with a powerful
                    "hand brake.   The vehicle would contain two 3rd
                    "Class compartments, one 1st Class compartment
                    "(accommodation for 22 passengers) and the
                    "Guard and Luggage compartment, where the brake
                    "is fixed.   The Tractor has also a powerful brake."

          If this would be permissible, a better passenger

service could be arranged on the section.

          Thanking you in anticipation for an early reply,

          I am, Sir,

                    Your obedient Servant,

                                             SUPERINTENDENT.

A two page letter in which Capt. May introduces the Ministry of Transport to the idea of operating the branch with a petrol tractor.   He drops a less than subtle hint that unless this is agreed to they may have to discontinue the passenger service.

5411

MINISTRY OF TRANSPORT,
7, Whitehall Gardens,
London, S.W.1.

11th January, 1924.

Dear Sir,

        With reference to your letter of the 4th January addressed
to the Ministry regarding your proposal to utilise a Simplex tractor,
I shall be much obliged if you will let me know what the weight of
the tractor is.   I presume it is of the 4-wheeled type.   At the
same time, would you kindly describe the type of brake with which it
is fitted, whether hand or power or both, and the number of blocks
operating on the wheels.   If you have a drawing of the tractor
I should be glad to see it, ~~showing the braking equipment.~~

        In regard to the bogie vehicle to be used with the tractor,
I presume that you propose to fit this with a hand brake operating a
block on each wheel.   Would you let me know if this is the case, *or
whether it would be practicable to operate the brake continuously with
and from the tractor.*
        In regard to the existing steam worked trains, I shall be
glad if you will let me know what the braking equipment is, and
whether a power brake is fitted, continuous throughout the train, and
whether it is of the vacuum or Westinghouse type.

                                    Yours faithfully,

                                    A.H.L. Mount.

                                    Lieut.Colonel.

John May Esq.,
    Superintendent,
        Welsh Highland Railway,
        Portmadoc.

*P.S. At terminals, I presume that the
intention is to run round the vehicle, so
that no journey will be made with the
vehicle running in front of the tractor?*

AM/DMB.

*A cautious response from Col. Mount for the Ministry to Capt. May,
seeking further information.   The FR has forgotten to change the
month on the 'Received' date stamp!*

AM/DMB

M/963/ED   18th January,   24

Lieut.-Colonel A.H.L. Mount,
      Ministry of Transport,
        7, Whitehall Gardens,
          LONDON, S.W.1.

Dear Sir,

          With reference to your letter of the 11th instant,
I enclose herewith a blue print of the Tractor and also
a specification of same, which I have just received from
the makers.   These, I think, will give full particulars.

          As regards the vehicle to be used with the Tractor,
this is what we describe as a "Combined Bogie Van," weighing
6 tons.   It contains, as stated in my letter, three compart-
ments, which can accommodate 22 passengers, a luggage
compartment, and also a compartment for the guard.   The Van
is fitted with a powerful hand screw brake operating a block
on each of the eight wheels.   It is not practicable to
operate the brake continuously and from the Tractor.
The couplings on the Tractor and vehicle are strong centre
couplings.   If it was permitted to use the Tractor, no
journey would be made except with the Tractor in front.

          The existing steam-worked trains have the continuous
brake, viz. on the Festiniog Railway, Vacuum, and on the Welsh
Highland Railway, Westinghouse type.   Engines are also
provided with hand brake; so are the Guard's vans.

                    Yours faithfully,

ENCL:

Capt. May provides the information that Col. Mount is seeking, making it clear
that the 'tractor' will be pulling the train and not pushing it and that the coach
they intend to use is known as a 'Combined Bogie Van' capable of seating 22
passengers.

5931

ENCLOSURE No 102

Highland Railway.

Telegrams,
FLUXODE, DOLGARROG.

National Telephone,
20 TYN-Y-GROES (Llandudno)

YOUR REFERENCE

OUR REFERENCE
WHICH KINDLY GIVE IN YOUR REPLY.

M/Box/1/ED

HJJ/BL.

Chairman's Office:-
Clark Street.
Dolgarrog. 28th. Jan. 1924
NORTH WALES.

29. JAN. 1924
RECEIVED

Superintendent,
    Festiniog Railway Company,
    PORTMADOC.

Dear Sir,

                        LIST OF LETTERS.

        Replying to yours of the 24th. instant, I should be
glad, if in future, when there is a blank, if you will be
kind enough to insert "Nil" or "error".

        I note the correspondence with the Ministry of Transport,
and hope you receive consent to use this arrangement, but
I do not think it altogether wise to make the statement
contained in your letter of the 4th. instant.

        It has always seemed to me that we ought to use a Tractor
to run our passenger service on the Bryngwyn Branch, and the
same Vehicle would I think handle the goods traffic. Will
you please let me know what the grades on this branch are, and
what objections there are to using a tractor.

        I return the file herewith.

        I also return the file of correspondence with the P.O.
Engineering Department.

                        Yours faithfully,
            FOR THE WELSH HIGHLAND RAILWAY COMPANY

                                        CHAIRMAN.

The chairman, Henry Joseph Jack, now gets involved and whilst cautioning Capt. May about his 'possibly withdrawing passenger services' statement in his first letter to the Ministry lends his support to the proposal with a particular reference to the 'Tractor' running the passenger services on the Bryngwyn branch.

6012

Telegraphic Address :
"TRANSMINRY, PARL, LONDON.
Telephone No.: VICTORIA 8660.

Any further communications should
be addressed to—
THE ASSISTANT SECRETARY,
SECRETARIAL DEPARTMENT,
MINISTRY OF TRANSPORT,
6, WHITEHALL GARDENS, S.W.1,
and the following reference quoted :—

S.R.2194.
....

MINISTRY OF TRANSPORT,

SECRETARIAL DEPARTMENT,

6, WHITEHALL GARDENS,

LONDON, S.W.1.

7th February, 1924.

Sir,

      With reference to your letter of the 4th
January, respecting the proposal to work passenger
trains on your Company's Railway by means of a Simplex
Tractor instead of a Steam Locomotive, I am directed
by the Minister of Transport to call attention to the
requirements of Section 1 (c) of the Regulation of
Railways Act, 1889, as to the provision of continuous
brakes on all trains carrying passengers and to inquire
how the Company propose to meet this obligation with
the type of tractor in question.

      I am, Sir,
      Your obedient Servant,

E. L. Rowntree.

The Superintendent,
  Welsh Highland Railway
    (Light Railway) Company,
    Portmadoc,
      North Wales.

EBB.

*A new man from the Ministry, Mr Rowntree, now replies to Capt. May.   He asks
quite pointedly how the company proposes to meet the requirement that all passenger trains must have a continuous braking system when using the petrol tractor.
The FR have now got the date stamp right!*

S.R 2194

M/963/ED   19th February, 24

The Assistant Secretary,
    Secretarial Department,
        Ministry of Transport,
            6, Whitehall Gardens,
                LONDON, S.W.1.

Sir,

    With reference to your letter of the 7th instant,
seeing that there would never be more than one vehicle attached
to the Motor, and that both the motor and the vehicle would
be provided with brakes to all wheels, it was not proposed
to provide continuous brakes as well.

    The Driver would have control of the brake on the
motor and the guard would control the brake on the vehicle,
which would be attached.

        I am, Sir,

           Your obedient Servant,

Capt. May, having thought about the Ministry's question for some two weeks during which time he would have consulted his colleagues, is struggling to find an appropriate response to the Ministry's question about continuous braking. Having explained how the brakes will work he concedes that "it was not proposed to use continuous brakes as well"

6913

MINISTRY OF TRANSPORT,

Telegraphic Address :
" TRANSMINRY, PARL, LONDON."
Telephone No. VICTORIA 8660.

Any further communications should
be addressed to—
THE ASSISTANT SECRETARY,
SECRETARIAL DEPARTMENT,
MINISTRY OF TRANSPORT,
6, WHITEHALL GARDENS, S.W.1,
and the following reference quoted :—

S.R.2194.

SECRETARIAL DEPARTMENT,

6, WHITEHALL GARDENS,

LONDON, S.W.1.

29th February, 1924.

Sir,

    With reference to your letter of the 19th
February, respecting the proposal to work passenger
trains on your Company's Railway by means of a
Simplex Tractor instead of a Steam Locomotive, I am
directed by the Minister of Transport to state that
he notes the information given, but that he is
advised that, in view of the gradients and other
special features existing on this light railway, the
Company could not properly be relieved from the
obligation to use continuous brakes on vehicles
carrying passengers on the line in question.

    I am, Sir,
      Your obedient Servant,

E. W. Rowntree

The Superintendent,
    Welsh Highland Railway
      (Light Railway) Company,
        Portmadoc,
          North Wales.

ELB

*Mr Rowntree again and in gentle civil servant 'speak' politely
tells Capt. May - "No, your proposal is unacceptable!"*

M/963/ED   3rd March,   24

Colonel H.F. Stephens, M.I.C.E.,
        Salford Terrace,
            TONBRIDGE.

Dear Sir,

                    USE OF TRACTOR FOR WORKING A PASSENGER
                    TRAIN ON W.H. RAILWAY.

            Referring to conversation with you some time ago
re working a brake coach on W.H. Railway with a tractor,
I enclose copy of the reply from Ministry of Transport for
your information.

            Can you arrange something to make the brake con-
tinuous?   If it was possible, it would save a good deal
of expense in the winter months.

                    Yours faithfully,

ENCL:

Capt. May, now like all managers, finds himself between a rock and and a hard place. Trying to reconcile the demands of his chairman and the implacable attitude of the Ministry of Transport he turns to that great Light Railway 'Fixer', Col Holman Stephens. He ask plaintively "Can you arrange something to make the brake continuous?"

FESTINIOG & WELSH HIGHLAND RAILWAYS.

6812

TELEGRAMS
STEPHENS, TONBRIDGE STATION.
PHONE: 143, TONBRIDGE.

ENGINEERS & LOCOMOTIVE SUPT'S. OFFICE,

Our Reference.   Your Reference.

SALFORD TERRACE,

FR.   B.

TONBRIDGE, KENT.

H. F. STEPHENS, *M.I.C.E.*

............8th March,.........1924..

Capt.J.May,
    Festiniog Railway,
        Portmadoc.

Dear Sir,

        Simplex Tractor working with
        Passenger Carriage.

        Yours of the 3rd instant.

        You might ask the Ministry of
Transport if they would agree to dispense
with the brake, if the Company invariably
undertook to run the Tractor at the rear
of the single coach when passing over steep
gradients, provided that efficient communication was arranged between the Guard, who
would ride in the first compartment, and
be provided with a look-out, and the driver
of the propelling Tractor.   As far as I can
see, otherwise, you will want a petrol-driver
air-pump, to exhaust the air from a chamber,
thus creating vacuum to work the brake.
I estimate the cost of this at £70. I do not
think you could work the ejector off the
exhaust from the petrol engine.

                Yours faithfully,

Col Stephens replies, and never short of ideas, suggests the solution of either the tractor pushing the coach or of installing a petrol-driven air pump.   Here the correspondence ends as Capt. May realises that he's run out of options.   But he has done his best!

6) Goods Workings

FORTUNATELY SEVERAL DRIVERS' logs have survived from the original Welsh Highland Railway and ten of these cover branch goods working in March 1928. These have enabled the goods train activities in WHR days to be accurately recorded

Typically the down goods would leave Bryngwyn with nineteen loaded slate wagons, one slab wagon, two empty open wagons, an occasional covered van and a brake van.

Down Trains		Up Trains	
Bryngwyn	4.00 pm	Dinas	2.00 pm
Tryfan Jct (arr)	4.25 pm	Tryfan Jct (arr)	2.15 pm
Tryfan Jct (dep)	4.29 pm	Tryfan Jct (dep)	2.19 pm
Dinas	4.40 pm	Bryngwyn	2.45 pm

At Dinas the slate was trans-shipped into standard gauge wagons for distribution via the national rail network. Other than to meet the requirements of local slate merchants, little use was being made of the once busy – for export – Caernarfon slate quays.

By 1928 the branch goods had been re-timed. Rather than departing from Dinas at 2.00pm the up train was scheduled to leave at 9.30am. It seldom left on time so that the 10.15 arrival at Bryngwyn was rarely achieved! Departing from Dinas the average train load would be eighteen wagons and a brake van. Of these eight would be slate empties – for working back up the incline – nine wagons of coal for the quarries and for the coal merchants at Rhostryfan and Bryngwyn – and a covered van for cement and bagged fertilizer. The coal would have been trans-shipped from standard gauge wagons using the tippler whilst dry goods would have been handled in the Dinas Goods Shed.

On average, four minutes was allowed for accessing the branch at Tryfan Junction and resetting the points for the main line. It is recorded that on

Top
The July 1923 working timetable is reproduced above.
This was a Monday to Friday service ; there were never any services on the Sabbath.

Left - transferring the slate from the narrow gauge wagons to the standard gauge ones at Dinas Junction in 1920 using manual labour.

Note the origins of the standard gauge wagons - London & North Western Railway and the Lancashire & Yorkshire Railway.

Topical Press

one occasion two covered wagon loads of 'manure' (i.e. fertiliser) were detached at Tryfan Junction presumably for unloading by local farmers. During this period both *Russell* and the *Baldwin/590* were being used on this 'turn' with Dafydd Lloyd Hughes as guard and 'Willie Hugh' Williams as driver. Both had been NWNGR employees, the latter having been with the railway since its inception.

The bulk of freight was destined for Bryngwyn, the quarries and coal merchants. However Rhostryfan would have additionally received substantial 'smalls' traffic for the local shops and community as well as coal. Unusually perhaps, the village had no hostelry and therefore no requirement for barrels of beer as on the main line. An interesting 'import' in an earlier period was special slate for making into writing slates at Bryngwyn mill.

At this period the branch goods was due back at Dinas in time for the engine to work the 12.45pm passenger train to Beddgelert. Thus with slate production reduced less time was required to work the incline. In 1921 Major Spring was tasked with assessing the assets and potential of the emerging WHR; in July and August of that year 411 and 633 tons of slate left Bryngwyn respectively and in July 178 tons of coal was carried up the branch.

At Dinas there were transfer wharves where slate was unloaded into standard gauge wagons while the other way coal was loaded into 4-ton wagons for delivery up the line. There were also 2-ton (2-plank) capacity wagons for sending coal up the incline where height was restricted beneath the Drumhead winding drum.

The carriage of explosives was noted with concern by the BoT as they were carried in metal cylinders in open wagons owned by the quarries. The BoT wanted vans but the railway stated that they were unsuited to the Bryngwyn

A goods train in Dinas yard comprised of a braked 4-ton coal wagon, WHR brake van, two empty slate wagons, three 2-plank coal wagons and a WHR covered van

(Commercial postcard)

incline as they would not fit under the winding drum. The BoT finally agreed to a maximum of five open wagons for explosives.

One unusual item of traffic was the removal of the steam locomotives *Lilla* (an 0-4-0 Hunslet now on the Festiniog Railway) and *Jubilee* 1897 (an 0-4-0 Manning Wardle (now in the Narrow Gauge Railway Museum at Tywyn) from the quarry at Cilgwyn after being sold to the Penrhyn slate quarry. The locos travelled on their own wheels down the Bryngwyn incline and on to Dinas where they were loaded onto the LMSR for transportation to Port Penrhyn.

The telephone wires between Dinas and the Drumhead were vital for notifying the number of wagons required by the quarries each day, but due to the exposed area through which the railway ran, they were liable to gale damage. Members of the permanent way gang were drafted in as unofficial linesmen to rectify the problems as and when they occurred.

Motive power in the early 1930s was provided by '*Moel Tryfan*' and '*Russell*' for the goods train but when the Welsh Highland Railway was opened to passengers throughout, the Baldwin '*590*' worked the goods. This was supplemented in 1928 by the Kerr Stuart prototype diesel 'tractor' which worked the branch for a short period. Goods trains were scheduled to run week days only.

When the quarry ceased sending traffic in 1935 the service was reduced to once a week for coal.

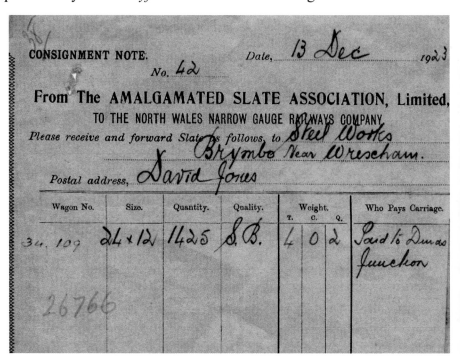

7) Quarry Feeder Tramways

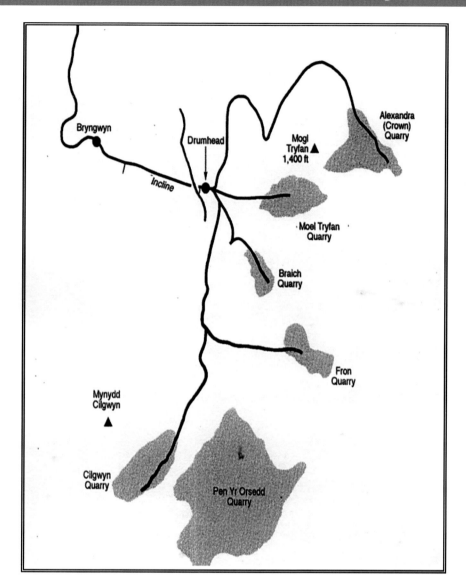

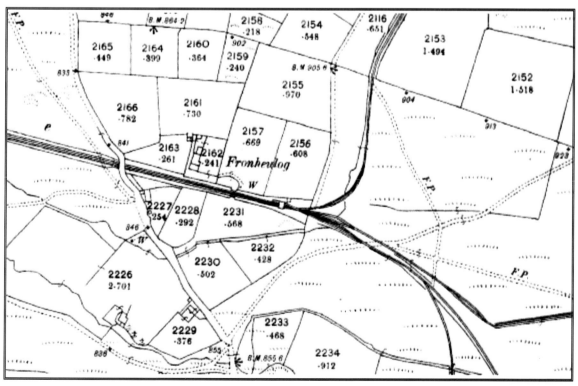

A T THE TOP of the Bryngwyn incline, known as the Drumhead, five feeder lines branched off to the various quarries.

Alexandra Slate Quarry

The Alexandra Slate Quarry was served by a 1½ mile long tramway designed by Charles Easton Spooner in 1876/7. It was laid out with long gradual climbs and a spectacular horseshoe curve. From the Drumhead the tramway headed off in a northerly direction climbing over 150 feet in the process.

The layout at the Drumhead consisted of a loop to stable wagons of slate that arrived from the quarry. Heading to the quarry the line entered a shallow cutting then with dry stone walls on either side it ran in a northerly direction climbing at 1in 50, rising to 1 in 30 on a 1¾ chain horseshoe curve to take it back on itself. Another horseshoe curve with a passing loop followed the contours round Moel Tryfan and finally, after a 30 foot high embankment, the quarry, a huge pit, was reached.

Motive power on the line included 'Kathleen' an 0-4-0 ST tank built by Vulcan Foundry and three vertical-boilered De Wintons. The quarries changed hands so it was not uncommon for the locomotives to be transferred from one quarry to another in the district. All track on the tramway was lifted in 1939.

The quarry, which had opened in 1861, used steam-powered mills and continued to expand thanks to the construction of the NWNGR to

A Ruston diesel shunter working in the Cilgwyn Quarry; note the use of the Blondin for lifting wagon loads of slate from the pit below.

Collection Gwynfor Pierce Jones

Bryngwyn complemented by opening of the tramway to the Drumhead and the Bryngwyn incline. At its peak the quarry produced over 6000 tons per annum, employed over 200 men and provided a great deal of slate traffic for the Branch. During World War I the quarry was closed but was later worked sporadically before finally closing in late 1934. Access was later gained to the Moel Tryfan slate quarry via a tunnel and slate was brought out until the 1960's by lorry.

Two members of the Welsh Railways Research Circle visit the quarries around Tryfan. Note the narrow gauge track still in place on the quarry feeder tramway to Alexander Quarry
Dave Southern

Moel Tryfan Slate Quarry

A second line left the Drumhead in an easterly direction on the level for 10 chains. This included two storage loops at the bottom of a double track incline to the quarry, 1250 feet up on the slopes of Moel Tryfan. Moel Tryfan quarry was an open pit working, with material coming out via a tunnel to the mill area. The finished goods left the quarry's slate mill for Dinas via the Drumhead and the incline.

In 1882 eighty one men produced 1880 tons of slate making it the third largest producer in the district. The quarry closed during World War I and in later years broke through into the Alexandra slate quarry workings via a tunnel. The quarry closed in 1935 with the final loads passing over the branch from the quarry to Dinas in February of that year. Consignment note - see right.

Small scale workings continued until the 1970's with rail operations ceasing in the quarry in September 1966 in

41

favour of road vehicles. Slate quarrying carried on intermittently until the 1980's. Tip reclamation providing ornamental slate for garden centres was observed in 2011.

Locomotives comprised low height variants of the Quarry Hunslet 0-4-0 ST design 'Tryfan' of 1902 and 'Cadfan' of 1904. Subsequently an 0-4-0 Ruston & Hornsby diesel was also used.

Braich Slate Quarry

A third quarry line was built in 1884 and ran from the Drumhead for 20 chains to a reversing neck which held two or three wagons; a short length of line to the quarry followed. Braich quarry was an open pit working developed in the 1820's when a water powered mill was built. Steam power was later introduced for pumping water out of the workings. Safe internal haulage was provided on a chain link incline. The output in 1882 was 2614 tons with one hundred and twenty four men employed. The quarry closed in 1911 but was taken over by the Amalgamated Slate Association Ltd who did little or no work and were eventually responsible for dismantling the quarry infrastructure.

Fron Slate Quarry

The fourth feeder line from the Drumhead gave access to Fron slate quarry which had opened in 1881. The line ran in a south westerly direction from the Drumhead between slate walls and fences, first on the east side then the west side of the road and finally alongside the main street in Fron village. It formed a junction opposite the post office with the line to Cilgwyn quarry.

Fron quarry was another open pit working with two pits linked by a tunnel. It used steam power for the mill and a cable incline. In 1883 the output was a mere 728 tons won by sixty-two men. Workings continued into the 1930's.

From the Drumhead a series of tramways fanned out to the various quarries.
This photograph shows such a tramway passing through Fron village.

Gwynedd Archive Services

Cilgwyn Quarry

The final of the five feeder lines, which included a storage loop, ran from the Drumhead in a southerly direction to Cilgwyn Quarry via the Fron quarry branch. The junction to Cilgwyn in the village of Fron was connected in 1923. (Photo page 40).

The slate workings at Cilgwyn date from the 14th century and were fully developed in the 18th century with four open pits. In 1882 the output was 7340 tons employing some three hundred men. Around 1933 traffic stopped using the Bryngwyn branch when the L.M.S. opened a new loading dock at Pen y Groes and slates went there by road. Originally, finished product was dispatched via the Nantlle Tramway to Caernarfon. The quarry finally closed in 1956.

Locomotives comprised three de Wintons, 'Lilla' and 'Jubilee' of previous mention and two diesel mechanical shunters.

From this it will be noted that the quarries were quick to take advantage of the coming of the railway. Nevertheless, this period was to prove to be the 'Indian summer' of the slate industry.

In 1918 the formation of the Amalgamated Slate Association brought Alexandra, Moel Tryfan, Braich and Cilgwyn quarries under common ownership.

'Llanfair' (above) is an example of a De Winton vertical boilered locomotive, built at the De Winton works in Caernarfon (opposite the current Welsh Highland terminus station) and used extensively in the quarries of North Wales. This example however is 2' 6" gauge and was used in the Penmaenmawr quarries. It is currently on display at Dinas station
David Allan

8) Working the Incline

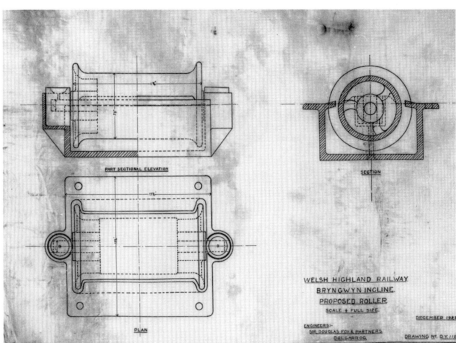

Top - The Drumhead at the top of Bryngwyn incline with cable still on the wooden drum. In the foreground is the termination of the double track incline. The point leads to a small yard from which the various tramways led to the Quarries. The scrapman has still to find his way here!
J.F. Bolton

Left - drawing of the proposed roller for the Bryngwyn incline by Sir Douglas Fox and Partners in December 1922. See photo on page 51.

BECAUSE SLATE WAS invariably won from mountainside quarries, inclines were the standard means for getting the products down onto the level to transport it away. The Bryngwyn incline with its double track and summit winding drum was a simple example of such a mechanism.

The wooden winding drum with a band brake was housed in the drum house at the Drumhead and adequately spanned the centre lines of the two incline tracks.   The wire haulage rope was wound onto the drum with each end serving one incline track.   Rope rollers were fitted to the centre of incline sleepers at intervals to prevent the haulage rope from dragging. (See photograph on p 51).   In 1924 new rollers were purchased costing £9-10s.   How many this sum represented is not known but they may well have been of the type illustrated (page 44) as recommended in 1922 by Sir Douglas Fox, consulting engineers to Sir Robert McAlpine who upgraded the NWNGR and built the WHR in 1922/23.   Wire rope oil was also purchased for the incline cable - £3-13s.   The official instructions for working the incline are reproduced as follows:-

Two abandoned slate wagons at the foot of the Bryngwyn incline in 1938.
D Mackereth

1. *The first four wagons down the incline must include two wagons with brakes which have been tested for safety purposes.*

2. *The winding drum and brake gear must be tested each day and any defects made good before being used.*

3. *The haulage cable must be examined on a weekly basis and greased and any defects regarding the drum, cable and brake gear must be reported to the staff at Dinas.*

4. *Loaded wagons when they arrive at the bottom of the incline must not be detached until their brakes have been pinned down.*

5. *Four sprags must be kept at the bottom of the incline and used as required.*

6. *Weighted catch points at the level crossing (at Bryngwyn station throat) examined and oiled before traffic worked.*

7. *Trainmen assisting in attaching and detaching wagons on the incline cable must ensure that there are enough wagons going up to compensate for the loaded wagons coming down*

Looking down the once bustling Bryngwyn incline from the Rhosgadfan road bridge to Bryngwyn station. The rails were lifted in 1941/42.
Bill Rear 1948

The importance of 6) was in case loaded slate wagons broke away from the incline cable and careered through the station towards the level crossing just beyond the signal cabin.

It was the train guard who trudged up the incline to operate the winding drum and help attach loaded wagons. At the incline foot the fireman was responsible for attaching/detaching wagons as appropriate. A quarry engine having brought loaded wagons to the Drumhead would signal by whistle what was on the way down; a long blast for empty coal wagons, short blast for loaded slate wagons while a continuous blast indicated a runaway. This often happened as former Welsh Highland driver Goronwy Roberts recalls. He tells the story of one of those inevitable breakaways in which he was involved when working the Bryngwyn

incline.   He remembers that he was driving *'Russell'* at the time when he heard the warning continuous whistle blast from the mist shrouded drumhead.   He swiftly put 'Russell' into reverse gear and backed off as eight wagons loaded with slate that had broken loose from the Drumhead at the top of the incline came hurtling down to derail at the bottom.   Adjacent to the bottom of the incline was a field of swedes.   Slates were scattered at random, some lodging in the swedes making them look like so many ice cream cones with wafers, and others upright in the field looking like headstones in a graveyard!

Most quarries needed to have inclines, but the NWNGR and its successor had an additional obstacle, the trans-shipment of slates to the standard gauge at Dinas.   As already mentioned as early as 1884 the NWNGR proposed an extension to Caernarfon and a Bryngwyn deviation, both to be separately funded but neither scheme came to fruition.   The alternative to the incline is interesting and merits further explanation.   It was planned to start at Bryngwyn station and in order to gain height on gradients suitable for adhesion working described two reverse curves in the process of which the existing incline would have been crossed twice.   A site near Fron post office was to become a reversing neck from where the line would have almost paralleled the rising formation to reach the drumhead at 90° to the incline.

A Sailing ship moored to the slate quay in Caernarfon harbour.   Standard gauge wagons loaded with slates that may well have come from Brynwyn and been trans-shipped at Dinas Junction await unloading.

Welsh Highland Heritage Group

9) Accidents & Incidents – Early Recollections

O F THESE THERE were many over the years but there is only one recorded fatality. Of the other accidents few merited reporting to the BoT. Slate wagons derailing was a perennial problem and it is perhaps not surprising that they were involved with the fatality.

Quarry loco 'Kathleen' with driver Richard Cunnah in charge

(Unknown)

In December 1901 on a Friday afternoon in fading light, driver Richard Cunnah brought the last loaded train of slate wagons from Alexandra Quarry to the Drumhead hauled by engine *'Kathleen'*. NWNG guard and sometime Bryngwyn stationmaster Robert Hughes was helping with the shunting at the top of the incline to help get his train away. He got his foot trapped between two rails while controlling a full slate wagon by walking in front of it but with his back to it acting as a human brake. He became stuck and despite the efforts of a co-worker to prevent the wagon from running over him received crush injuries to his leg which proved to be fatal. A group of quarrymen having just finished work provided a stretcher party down to Bryngwyn and Dr Williams of 'Tryfan' attended but Robert Hughes sadly died around 8.00pm that night.

On the 14th February 1896 the 4.50pm mixed train from Bryngwyn had progressed but half a mile when a wheel loose on its axle caused the derailment of six wagons loaded with slates. The four empty coal wagons and bogie brake composite coach at the rear stayed on the line. This would not be the only occasion when the BoT had to remind the railway

that with mixed trains passenger stock must be marshalled next to the engine.

A more human story involved Rhostryfan farmer Morris Davies, who, in October 1877 (not long after the opening of the branch) was found guilty at Caernarfon County Court of assaulting Ellen Jones, the wife of a neighbouring farmer.   Judge Horatio Lloyd awarded her two guineas (£2-2/-) damages.   Both parties had been visiting the Caernarfon Eisteddfod and shortly after leaving Dinas Davies and others in the carriage started smoking.   Being of ill health the plaintiff requested them to desist and all complied except Davies, who allegedly remarked that he hated women and would do all he could to annoy them, puffed pipe smoke in her face.   Ellen tried to hook the pipe out of his mouth with her umbrella which Davies wrested from her and with it beat her about the head and face.   Davies had been provoked by the umbrella incident and the judge's opinion was that he should have simply returned the umbrella.   (Perhaps in 1877 there was no opportunity for a 'No Smoking' carriage?!).

John Paull, a slate merchant with a stacking area on Caernarfon quay would, from recorded information, appear to have been a devious character.   In 1897 he was making a claim in the Chancery Division of the High

Ponies still graze on the trackbed today.   One of whom is pictured here looking through the original NWNG gate between the original NWNG slate gateposts at a minor level crossing on the up side of Rhostryfan station.

David Allan

SLIDING   FIXED

Court for £15 relating to the loss or non-delivery by the railway company of slates more than four years previously!

Furthermore he was claiming £8 for the loss of a pony which had been grazing with others on common land adjacent to the branch. Somehow Paull's pony and another had got onto the railway track when Owen Thomas, guard-cum-station master on the branch was gravitating down to the junction on a 'trolley'. They ran along the track in front of him and disappeared. On reaching a bridge over a small stream, Thomas found Paull's pony dead *'having fallen with its front legs through spaces in the bridge and its nose in the water and so drowned'*. Russell, as the railway's Receiver and Manager opined that as the pony was a trespasser the action should be defended.

Perhaps Owen Thomas is best recalled for having kept a large number of caged birds (canaries?) in the Tryfan Junction signal box. 'O.T.' was good natured and would often give local children a ride on the trolley down to the junction. In the 1880s one of the Hafod Wernlas dogs would chase the trolley only to be pelted with stones stored on the trolley for the purpose. If there were ponies on the track O.T. would yell;
"lions, lions; bears, bears, what shall we do?".

The incline was a major source of wagon derailments – and the occasional 'runaway'. In 1931 Col Stephens was querying whether it was normal practice to attach wagon couplings to the incline rope with 'tarred string'!

Goronwy Roberts worked the branch with *'Russell'* and his 1988 recollection of working the incline is recorded here verbatim :-

"All the loaded wagons at the Drumhead belonged to the Welsh Highland. The name of the quarry engine was *'Kathleen'* and the name of the driver was Richard Cunnah. We had a mixed train going up to Bryngwyn with coal for the quarries and all that. And you would listen to the whistle on top. The fireman was at the bottom of the incline and I had to stay with my engine in case something happened and I was working to his

Top
Wrecked slate wagon at the bottom of the Bryngwyn incline in 1934 - possibly a runaway. The incline rollers are clearly visible between the rails near the top right hand corner of the picture.
Roger Kidner

Left
A youthful Goronwy Roberts in an earlier capacity as a stoker on the locomotive, before graduating to driver.
(Unknown)

instructions and hooking the wagons on. And the way we used to work was that the engine on top would whistle - two long and two short; two long and one short and that meant two coal wagons and one empty because if you had a heavier weight going up than coming down it would stop halfway (at a dip in the incline) and what would happen then the fireman would have to drag a thin wire rope, mind you it was a strong wire rope, hook it on to the ones that were coming down and hook it on to the back of my engine and then I had to pull them down. I wouldn't like to tell you the big words that were coming out then!! But it didn't happen very often."

Not only ponies strayed onto the line but also sheep. Farmers were compensated generally on the basis of £1 each. In 1884 one Thomas Llewelyn travelled the branch and visited the Alexandra Quarry. His edited report, published in the Liverpool Courier, is published below.

"Having travelled from Dinas to Rhyd Ddu, Mr Llewelyn was still left with the desire – again like many Victorians – to visit the 'sea beach' on Moel Tryfan "without a very large expenditure of time and trouble". Having previously made the acquaintance of Mr Robert Livesey, the energetic manager and secretary of the NWNGR, Mr Llewelyn was told that at least 500 ft in height and several miles of walking could be saved in the ascent by making use of the railway's Bryngwyn Branch. So at the next opportunity he took advantage of the facilities offered.

Narrow gauge track inside one of the slate sheds in the quarries. This carried the newly hewn rough slate blocks on the quarry wagons for the slate splitters to work on.

From Tryfan Junction the track diverges to the right with gradients 'often times varying from 1 in 35 to 1 in 30'. Rhostryfan, the first 'stoppage' on the branch is a flourishing and scattered village which, like others in the neighbourhood, appears to enjoy a creditable existence without numbering a single house of refreshment among its institutions (and so it remains today!).

After a further stretch of line the extent of the branch is gained at Bryngwyn. In the company of Mr Menzies, managing director of the 'Alexandra Slate Mining Company', Mr Llewelyn travelled from the Drumhead - having walked up the incline – to the quarry in a train of returned empty slate wagons hauled by one of the slate company's locomotives, possibly 'Kathleen'. This two mile journey was the steepest he had ever made on a railway with 1 in 35 gradients falling in places to 1 in 20 and 'chain and a half' curves that would not be allowed on a passenger line.

The train stopped at the slate dressing works on the way to the quarry presumably to drop off some empty slate wagons. Mr Llewelyn was impressed by the locomotive's ability to restart the train on the subsequent steep gradient. Eventually the quarry entrance was reached revealing an immense excavation from the brow of Moel Tryfan. There were four terraces or galleries making a total depth of 150 ft. The three lower ones are excavated in the slate and as is generally the case the lowest part of the quarry contains the best rock from which some very fine slates are split.

However, from a geological point of view, the 'upper wall' was of most interest being composed of 'incoherent sand and gravel'. This over burden has to be removed to spoil heaps before the slate can be won. Alas he was unrewarded in finding any sea shells!

Footnote - Note all measurements are as quoted and not necessarily accurate.

The slate dressing shed where possibly Mr Llewelyn stopped on his adventurous journey.

10) Bryngwyn Journey - an eyewitness account

This memoire, taken down verbatim, was written in about 1940 by John Hughes who had worked for the Welsh Highland Railway. It was translated from the Welsh by Myfannwy Roberts, wife of Goronwy Roberts who was both a driver and stoker on the line and whose memories feature in this book.

MR TANNER WAS one of the first General Managers; he built the house called "Fern Villa". Mr Tanner would frequently go to Bryngwyn on the train. However he had a handy trolley to travel back on which had been pulled by the train on the way up; this was a small four-wheeled wagon with a long brake handle.

The platelayers included - Big Will Roberts, the foreman, Jeff Lamerick, Sion Williams from Saron, Sam Bach from Saron and Sion Jones of Clochydd, Sam Jones from Chatam, Ted from Llangfadlan and Thomas Orr. (See photo on page 55).

In my time the guards were Twm Morris, who called himself "the passenger train man" and Owen Thomas, who was not only the guard on the Bryngwyn line but also the station master at Tyddyn Gwydd (Tryfan Junction). He went up on the train to Rhostryfan and Bryngwyn, and before the train returned he came back on the small trolley to prepare the lines at Tryfan Junction. He kept many birds at Tyddyn Gwydd, in the old signal box - very good singers all!

Robert Hughes was the Station Master at Bryngwyn, we used to call him Hughes Maen Coch. He was responsible for releasing the slate wagons on the big incline bringing slates from Foel, Gors y Bryniau, Braich and Fron quarries. Bryngwyn Station was an important and busy place when the quarries were at their peak. Mr Hughes had a fatal accident one evening at the top of the incline *(see full report on page 48)*. Dafydd Lloyd got his place and kept it for a number of years.

Perhaps I can describe for you a trip by the little train from Dinas to Bryngwyn. We leave Dinas at 9.00am, *'Moel Tryfan'* is the engine; the

A loaded coal wagon waits in the siding whilst the coal merchant's scales lurk against the rear fence. A barrel seems to have been left where it was rolled off the wagon.
(Courtesy Snowdon Mountain Railway)

train is made up of two carriages - part of one of them is first class, then a covered van carrying flour and goods, followed by a large coal-carrying wagon and sixteen empty slate wagons and finally, a guards van. The first class compartment is occupied by someone going to the Moel Tryfan Company and a Mr Menzies for Gors y Brynniau. There are several other including two Jewish men who are going to the quarries to sell watches at lunchtime. There's also an old gentleman from Waen Wen selling ointment, excellent stuff for getting rid of warts.

We take our seats and set off. At Dinas we pass the smithy, the carpenters shed, the foundry and the signal box before going into Glanrhyd cutting and then under the main Pwllheli and Porthmadog road bridge. We soon arrive at the Pont Cae Moel bridge. This bridge goes over the river and under the Rhos Isaf road. On the next stretch there are many gates that can be seen from the train for the fields and stiles for the footpaths.

The train goes over a well-made bridge at the bottom of Bodaden farmyard. Fencing now encloses the track as far as Wernlasddu bridge. Then it's under the Tir Caehen bridge quickly followed by Bicall bridge before arriving at Tyddyn Gwydd (Tryfan Junction). At Tyddyn Gwydd Station, Owen Thomas unloads some small parcels from the train and puts them in his office in the station. We collect two more passengers who are going to Bryngwyn. The guard attaches the trolley to the back of the train and off we go.

Thomas Orr (left), one of the platelayers mentioned by John Hughes in his memoire, and another un-named ganger on their trolley on the branch in 1934.
The rope held by the right hand man would have been used for attaching the trolley to the rear of the train.

Photo courtesy Mrs Ruth Strello

We take the right hand track at the points for Rhostryfan and Bryngwyn, with the other line going to Rhyd Ddu. We pass under another bridge with the road above going to various farms. By Cae Hen gates we stop, the rails are wet with dew, and the fireman goes to sit on the front buffer of the engine to release sand on the rails – this is his job from here to Bryngwyn. The sand does its work and we move on quite steadily. At Rhostryfan Station, we pass a signal box, a goods siding, a large waiting room, a ticket office and the goods warehouse.

Rhostryfan Station is very convenient, as it is almost in the village and it's also handy for Rhosgadfan. A lot of goods are often unloaded at Rhostryfan Station; customers include Jones Hughes, Evan Griffiths of Bryn Crin, and William Jones. There are items for Fourcrosses, which need to go on by cart. A wooden building (warehouse) is by the station gate with access from the road to the school. This houses scales for weighing wagons and also platform type machines.

As we set off from Rhostryfan we can see coal wagons behind the station in the siding. Under a bridge from Dir Cae Rhug and then the old Wmffra bridge. The road from Rhosgadfan crosses the line in the centre of the village. There are many gates from here on and many small bridges over streams. We pass Ty Rallt and head for Hen Dy Newydd, then we are on an embankment and we cross a well-built bridge over the river at Caehaidd Bach Marshes. Caehaidd Terrace now comes into sight and we cross the Afon Wen by a large bridge. Water, supplying hundreds of houses, now flows from Ffynnon Wen, with a water pipe going as far as Dinas Dinlle.

Elwyn Jones on one of the prominent embankments above Rhostryfan. The embankments is pierced by one of the well-constructed bridges or culverts (left hand corner) mentioned by John Hughes The sleeper marks remain even after 50 years
David Allan

The train is now in a deep cutting not far from Bryngwyn. Then follows a rather sharp turn and we cross the fast flowing river by another well-built bridge. The little train slows down as there are many mountain ponies in the Station area. The guard goes ahead to herd them off the track and steam from the whistle from old Penbont encourages them into a gallop. We cross the road from Carmel by a level crossing with the gates closed across the road on both sides and we arrive at Bryngwyn station - a busy and important place.

The train provides an essential service for neighbouring areas with the quarries bringing in most revenue. We find ourselves in an open area with extensive sidings, including a long coal siding. Bryngwyn has a signal box, an explosives store, an office for Mr Hughes the Station Master, a large waiting room next to the goods depot, and another large goods store with a high platform for unloading goods and flour. The coal siding is full of wagons and waiting for a chat we see Robert Thomas of Bryngwyn, John Roberts of Carmel, Evan from Bwlchllyn, and Bob Siop of Fron. Everyone seems to be busy. There is a wagon for Tomos Elias, who's coming for boxes of goods, and the weighing machine, the same as the one at Rhostryfan, is very busy at the foot of the incline.

Today we are delivering a new locomotive for the Foel Quarry. This one had a special train to bring it up from Dinas. There is a great fuss, and we're almost ready to start. It's attached to the wire rope and Hughes is at the top of the incline by the drum. He begins raising it slowly but after 100 yards it stops and after enquiring we find that the men have to manoeuvre the engine to enable it to go under the middle of Fronheulog bridge. It then continues successfully on its way up the incline. *Kathleen'* is the name of the small Gors-y-Bryniau engine that pulls it up to the Foel Quarry tracks.

There have been many accidents on the incline with couplings or axles snapping as they travelled down the incline at great speed, and all this represents losses to the little railway company.

There are two trains daily to Bryngwyn, one in the morning and the other in the afternoon but on Saturdays there are four or five journeys. If I can remember rightly the first on Saturday is at about 8.00am, they called it the market train. The last train would arrive at Bryngwyn at about 8pm or 9pm.

We are most grateful to Alun Turner for permission to publish this extract

11) Motive Power

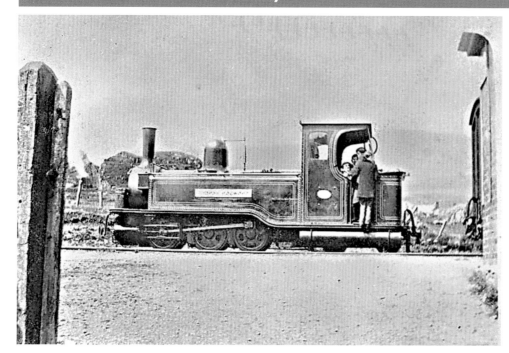

Left
'Snowdon Ranger'
photographed at Rhyd Ddu
(John Keylock collection)

Bottom
Passengers and foot-plate crew pose in front of 'Moel Tryfan' as she awaits departure from Bryngwyn with a bogie brake composite.
A tangle of wire rope and miscellaneous bits of equipment would no doubt be officially designated as a trip hazard today.
(Unknown)

'MOEL TRYFAN' AND *'Snowdon Ranger'* were identical 0-6-4T Single Fairlie engines built by Vulcan Foundry of Newton le Willows and delivered to the N.W.N.G.R. in 1875.

Designed by George Percival Spooner they had a 6-coupled power bogie under the boiler and a 4-wheeled one under the cab. The front coupling was attached to the bogie frame which also carried the cylinders with Stephenson's valve gear. In 1917, with the continuing financial constraints of the day as well as wartime conditions, the frames of *'Snowdon Ranger'* were put under *'Moel Tryfan'* to make one good engine. The remains were scrapped.

'Gowrie' was another 0-6-4T but built by Hunslet Engine Co of Leeds in 1908 for the anticipated extension of the railway from Rhyd Ddu to Beddgelert. It was the last Single Fairlie built.

'Beddgelert' an 0-6-4 saddle tank with outside frames and cylinders, was also built by Hunslets in 1878 specifically for use on the Bryngwyn branch. It was constructed with its boiler sloping slightly upwards towards the front thus allowing the engine to run cab first uphill with wagons trailing behind the smoke box where the overhang was less. This reduced the risk of derailment and maintained boiler water level on the steep inclines of the branch.

Top
The NWNG loco, 0-6-4 saddle tank, 'Beddgelert' at Dinas - specially built for the branch with its inclined boiler.
Symons Gems of Wales

Left
0-6-4T 'Gowrie' with a freight train at Dinas.   A ganger's trolley waits to be attached by rope to the brake van at the rear of the train.
FR Archives

'**Russell**'a 2-6-2 Side Tank, was built by Hunlet of Leeds for the Portmadoc, Beddgelert and South Snowdon Railway but delivered to the N.W.N.G.R. in 1906.   Even though the railway was not finished the engine was bought because the locomotives on the N.W.N.G.R were showing their age and were not powerful enough for the anticipated extended line to Beddgelert. *Russell'* arrived and became the engine of choice for Bryngwyn branch duties.   She was known to have worked the Bryngwyn branch during 1924-25, 1928 and 1934.   She was originally painted Midland Red but later the colour was changed to light green following the lease of the line to the Festiniog Railway.

Top
'Russell' with a goods train outside the goods shed at Dinas in 1933
Bottom
A rather murky photograph shows 'Russell' heading for Bryngwyn at a somewhat dilapidated Rhostryfan station.   The only known photograph of 'Russell' on the branch
HM Comber/FR Archives

Baldwin '590' 4-6-0T was built at the Baldwin Locomotive Works, Philadelphia USA in 1917 for use on the Western Front during World War I. The engine was purchased from the Government Property Disposals Board by Col Stephens, FR & WHR Engineer & Manager from 1923-1931, and arrived at Dinas in July 1923 having cost £240.

Prototype Diesel Tractor - a six-wheel diesel tractor built by Kerr Stuart & Co No 4415 in 1928 arrived at Dinas in July 1928 and worked the Bryngwyn branch until being transferred to the Festiniog Railway in March 1929. She was noted as not being popular with crews being slow and once it started to slip it would stall and tend to derail. The engine later found its way to the Union Vale Sugar factory in Mauritius from where it was repatriated and is now awaiting restoration in the Minffordd yard of the FR.

Top 4-6-0T Baldwin '590' in the Aberglaslyn Pass
Bill Minnion

*Left
Pioneering Kerr Stuart diesel loco that worked the Bryngwyn branch for several months as a trial*
Tom Rolt

12)   The In-Between Years

BY MAY 1937 all activity on the WHR had ceased, the last passenger trains having been run the previous September. The station buildings at Rhostryfan and Bryngwyn had already started to show signs of dilapidation due to lack of use; in WHR days Tryfan Junction had been but an unstaffed halt. 'Russell' and Baldwin '590' languished in the Dinas engine shed and 'Moel Tryfan' stayed at the FR's Boston Lodge works where it had been for 'repair' since 1935.

Then came World War II and with it a drive for 'scrap' metal to fuel the war effort. To this end the whole railway was requisitioned under the government's emergency defence regulations – George Cohen and Sons being awarded the demolition contract. This national company were well known machinery and scrap metal merchants. Track lifting on the branch started in January 1942 progressing to the junction and back to Dinas. Rail, sleepers and carriages were offered for sale, '590' was cut up but fortunately 'Russell' survived to find an initial home at the open cast iron ore mines in Oxfordshire. The resultant trackbed reverted to nature and was encroached upon

Top
'590' submits to the gasman's axe at Dinas in 1937
A.E. Rimmer
Below
1942 and the rails on the branch above Rhostryfan are being lifted to aid the war effort
A.E. Rimmer

and utilised by adjacent landowners. The three station buildings were vandalised for their reusable stone, slate and timber. By 1947 a new road bridge had been built across the Bryngwyn incline and by the 1980s Tryfan Junction station building was difficult to find!

The branch's salvation came in 1995 with the acquisition of the whole WHR trackbed by the FR. In 2004 most of the trackbed between Rhostryfan and Bryngwyn was opened as a permissive footpath and became part of the 'slate trail'. The section from Tryfan Junction to Rhostryfan was opened in March 2011.

Top
A barely recognisable jumble of granite marks the site of Bryngwyn station in 2008. The Ruabon yellow brick corners, characteristic of the NWNG buildings, still remain to identify the corner of the building.
David Allan

Left
73 years after the branch closed Michael Davies fights his way through the heavy growth of brambles that covered the trackbed on the approach to Rhostryfan station
David Allan

13) Walking the Bryngwyn Branch today - The Slate Trail Footpath

WHEN THE WELSH Highland Railway track bed came into ownership of the Festiniog Railway there were no plans to reinstate the Bryngwyn branch as a railway line. The FR leased the majority of the track bed to Gwynedd County Council who in turn leased it to Llanwnda Community Council who proposed to make it into a permissive footpath.

The railway supported the idea with the provision that it would not hinder the reinstatement of the railway in the future. The distance of the walk along the Branch from Tryfan Junction to the top of the incline at the Drumhead and back is approximately six miles. Many of the features encountered will have been mentioned in the earlier route description.

Funding for the first section of the footpath was secured by Llanwnda Community Council from the Slate Valleys Initiative Scheme which was part of a programme for the regeneration of Gwynedd's slate quarrying districts. Work started in February 2002 between Rhostryfan and the first level crossing on the approach to Bryngwyn but not including the horseshoe curve around Bryngwyn farm on the approach to Bryngwyn station site. In July 2006 bilingual interpretation panels were added giving details of the route.

Local councillor Alun Ffred Jones cuts the ribbon on the 21st May 2011 at Rhostryfan to open the first stage of the footpath that utilises the old branch. It was later named 'The Slate Trail'.

David Allan

On leaving the platform at Tryfan Junction note the information panel and follow the lane heading towards the gated entrance to Tyddyn Gwydd farm. The entrance to the farm is on the original route of the Bryngwyn branch alongside which a footpath has been created which is entered by a kissing gate adjacent to the farm gate. As the farm access goes left we are now on the Branch proper, it turns through a 180° curve and is tree-lined on either side. The path passes under the minor road with the brick arch lined in yellow Ruabon brick.

Top - the bridge carries the old road to Rhosgadfan over the trackbed, its characteristic North Wales Narrow Gauge yellow brick and granite architecture still dominate the trackbed
David Allan

Left - the same yellow Ruabon brick outlines the little bridge that carries the track, now footpath, over the tumbling waters of the Afon Rhyd
Dave Southern

Within yards we pass over the Afon Rhyd and again the brick arch is lined in yellow brick and can be seen on either side from a public footpath which crosses the trackbed at this point. From here the line passes through open countryside until the site of Rhostryfan station is reached.   Up to this point the trackbed had received a crushed slate surface and improved fencing and drainage.   From the site of Rhostryfan station good views of the Menai Straits and Anglesey can already be had.

The station site has now been landscaped and grassed over, with picnic tables and bench provided. A slate slab platform incorporating the original slate platform edging and a replica station sign have been installed. The section of the former trackbed from here to the village High Street has been the subject of a further grant to Llanwnda Community Council from the Welsh Government for its incorporation into the slate trail footpath.

 This section was opened in 2012 and included complete fencing on either side, clearance of the track bed and the provision of slate waste for its surface. From the station the track bed passes through a shallow cutting which is crossed by a disused stone footbridge, again with the arch lined with yellow brick. After the bridge the track bed rises, crosses a stream and meets the High Street whereas formerly the railway went under the road.   The High Street is gained by a kissing-gate with wheelchair access. Hereafter all further gates have provision for disabled access.

The new sign post directs walkers along the Slate Trial, but a very much earlier rail-built style affords an easier access over the line's boundary wall in operational days.

Dave Southern

Across the road is a similar gate, slate trail signs and descriptive board. At the start of this section the trackbed has been filled in to meet road level. Dropping down to the original level the path passes between houses and a field before reaching the crossing of a minor road (Tyddyn Canol) where the original level crossing gates are still in situ. From here the trackbed has been recently fenced (2013) and surfaced with crushed slate waste. The path soon crosses a further minor road after which it enters open countryside. An original rail-built ladder stile still exists and the path, now on an embankment, crosses a significant culvert before reaching the site of an old waterworks on the left. Cae Haidd Terrace then appears on the right, with another minor road crossing adorned with information boards.

The path enters a gentle right hand curve representing the start of a horseshoe around Bryngwyn 'farm'. This is not currently accessible (2013) as it is in the custody of an adjacent Community Council and cannot be used until fenced.

Therefore turn left onto the next lane, pass the drive to Bryngwyn Farm and, having taken a 90° bend, you will see the branch on your right. The minor road crossed the trackbed and just beyond is the remains of Bryngwyn station on land now in private ownership.

To gain access to the incline go past the old station and take the first footpath on the left and follow it to where it comes out opposite Capel y Bryn. Turn

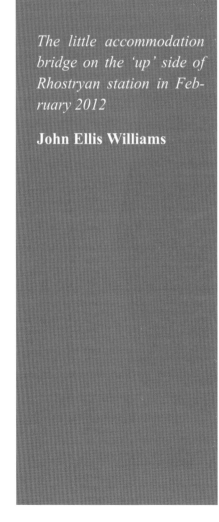

The little accommodation bridge on the 'up' side of Rhostryan station in February 2012

John Ellis Williams

The dramatic Moel Tryfan quarry. This is in private ownership and is out of bounds to the general public

Dave Southern

left on a minor road which crosses the incline and gain access here. Follow the incline up the hill to a wall which is alongside the Rhosgadfan to Fron road. Turn right and you will see the steps leading up to the road. Turn left to view the old road bridge which passes over the incline while the present road is built through it.

To view the Drumhead retrace your steps and walk back along the road and take a track on the left to the top of the incline and you will shortly see a display board showing the sites of the quarries and the routes of the tramways to them. The Drumhead was the cable winding house for the incline and can be seen from the track but is on private property not accessible to the public. If you turn around the marshy area in front of you was where there were sidings and loops and the start of various tramways to the quarries. Behind one can see the tips of the quarries and if one is tempted to explore them we must remind you that they are private property with no public right of way. They have not been active for many years with the exception of the main Moel Tryfan/ Alexandra quarry which saw some revival in 2007.

If one has started the walk from Tryfan Junction just retrace your steps and enjoy the views of the Menai Straits and Anglesey on your return.

With car parking at Tryfan Junction being limited arrival there by train is to be recommended. As it is a 'request' halt be sure to tell the guard that you wish to alight at Tryfan Junction. At the platform approach there is an information board containing a timetable which will state the time of the return trains. To stop a train simply give the appropriate hand signal.

Further Reading

Industrial Locomotives of North Wales V.J.Bradley

Industrial Railway Society. (1922)

Cwm Gwyrfai G.P.Jones & A.J. Richards. Carreg Gwalch. 2004

Narrow Gauge Railways in South Caernarfonshire
J.I.C.Boyd Oakwood Press 1972

The Welsh Highland Railway J.I.C.Boyd Oakwood Press 1989

Illustrated History of the WHR Peter Johnson O.P.C. 2009

Various issues of the WHR Heritage Magazine

Caernarfon Record office files

Russell - Andrew Neale WHR Ltd 1996

"To stop a train simply give the appropriate hand signal"

A glorious shot of KI on a 'double-header' at Tryfan Junction

Derek Buckles

PostScript - as the first edition of this book goes to press we learn that there is a plan to reconstruct Bryngwyn station building as a holiday home. This follows a big increase in visitors to the area calling at the house adjacent to the old building which has inspired the owners to enter planning discussions with the County Council. So the story goes full circle!

This dramatic satellite picture show the scars left on the face of Snowdonia by the quarries in the Moel Tryfan area. Most of the high quality slate extracted from these quarries would have been carried down the two foot track of the Bryngwyn branch of the Welsh Highland Railway.
Picture courtesy of Bing Maps

The Authors

Left
Dave Southern - author of several railway books, a member of the Welsh Highland Heritage Group and a key volunteer in the reconstruction of Tryfan Junction station building. Not unsurprisingly Dave lists 'walking' as being amongst his hobbies!

Below
John Keylock - a member of the Welsh Highland Railway almost since its inception in 1964; he was a founder member of the Welsh Highland Heritage Group and its secretary from its inception in 1997. His boundless enthusiasm for the heritage of the Welsh Highland was quite simply inspirational.

This book has been jointly written by Dave Southern and John Keylock. Inspired by Dave Southern's examination of the noticeboard erected at the entrance to the current Tryfan Junction station Dave realised that the time was ripe for a book on the Bryngwyn branch. Designed as the main route in 1874 of the NWNGR it was eventually demoted to a mere sideline as the Welsh Highland evolved on different route to that planned by its promoters.

The branch clung on to life almost until the end of the railway's operation and now thanks to John's inspirational leadership in the reconstruction of Tryfan Junction station it has secured a further lease of life as a footpath that enables today's passengers to walk the branch and to experience the wonderful Welsh countryside through which the little branch ran.

Unfortunately John died before the work was completed and it has been my task to try and understand how he might have wanted the finished book to look. I've done my best!

David Allan